JOURNEY THROUGH
France

John Gamgee

Troll Associates

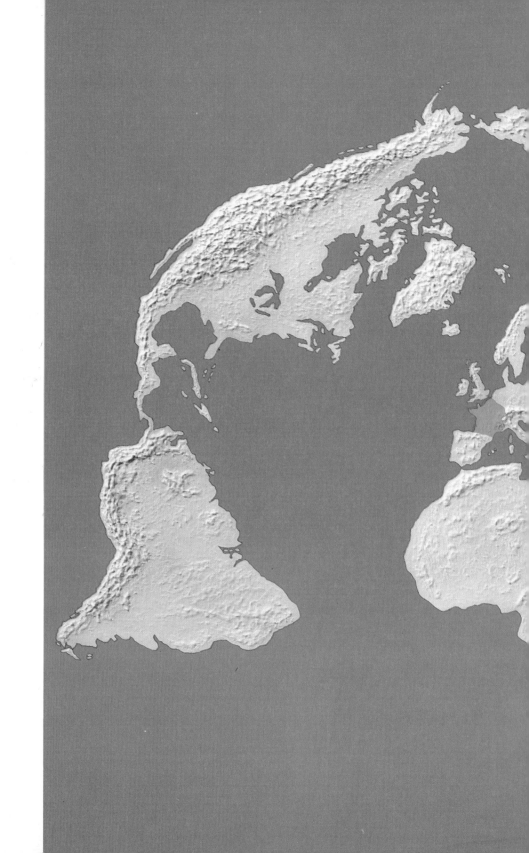

Library of Congress Cataloging-in-Publication Data

Gamgee, John, (date)
   Journey through France / by John Gamgee ;
illustrated by Chris Forsey ... [et al.].
      p.   cm.
   Includes index.
   Summary: Describes some distinct features of
life in France and, in particular, such cities as
Paris, Versailles, Lyon, Marseilles, and Le
Havre.
   ISBN 0-8167-2759-7 (lib. bdg.)
   ISBN 0-8167-2760-0 (pbk.)
   1. France—Juvenile literature.   [1. France.]
I. Forsey, Christopher, ill.   II. Title.
DC29.3.G36   1994
944—dc20   91-46175

Published by Troll Associates
© 1994 Eagle Books

Edited by Neil Morris and
Kate Woodhouse
Design by Sally Boothroyd
Picture research by Jan Croot

Illustrators: Martin Camm: 4, 5; Chris
Forsey: 21; Richard and Christa Hook: 23;
David More: 14, 26; Frank Nichols: 12; Mike
Roffe: 5; Ian Thompson: 4-5
Picture credits: Bridgeman Art Library: 10,
21; Colorsport: 15; Chris Fairclough: 24, 27;
David Howgrave-Graham: 6; Hutchison
Library/Timothy Beddow: 9; Hutchison
Library/Carlos Freire: 7; Hutchison Library/J.
Pate: 11; Hutchison Library/Leslie Woodhead:
18-19; Hutchison Library: 22; NHPA/Mignot-
Nature: 12-13; Christine Pemberton: 14-15, 18;
Spectrum: cover, 1, 7, 13, 16, 17, 19, 28-29, 29, 30;
Frank Spooner Pictures/Gamma: 25; ZEFA: 8,
9, 11, 16-17, 20-21, 22-23, 25, 26-27, 30

Printed in the U.S.A.
10 9 8 7 6 5 4 3 2 1

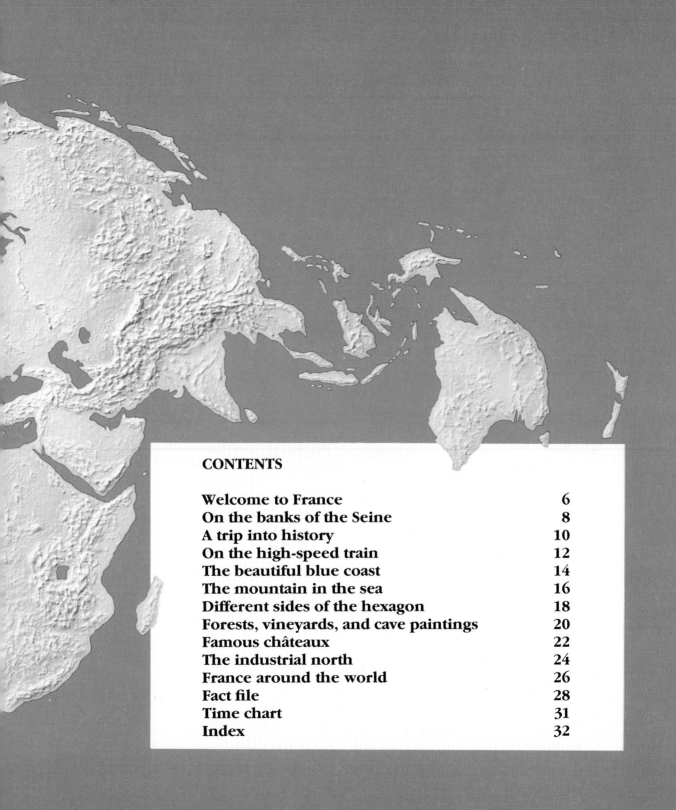

CONTENTS

France

KEY FACTS

Area: 211,208 sq. mi. (547,026 sq.km.)

Population: 56,411,000

Capital: Paris 8,707,000 people

Other major cities: Lyon 1,236,000
Marseille 1,116,000   Lille 946,000

Highest mountain: Mont Blanc 15,771 ft.
(4,807 m)

Longest river: Loire 650 mi. (1,050 km.)

Largest lake: Lake Geneva (Lac Léman) –
shared with Switzerland – 2245 sq. mi. (581 sq.km.)

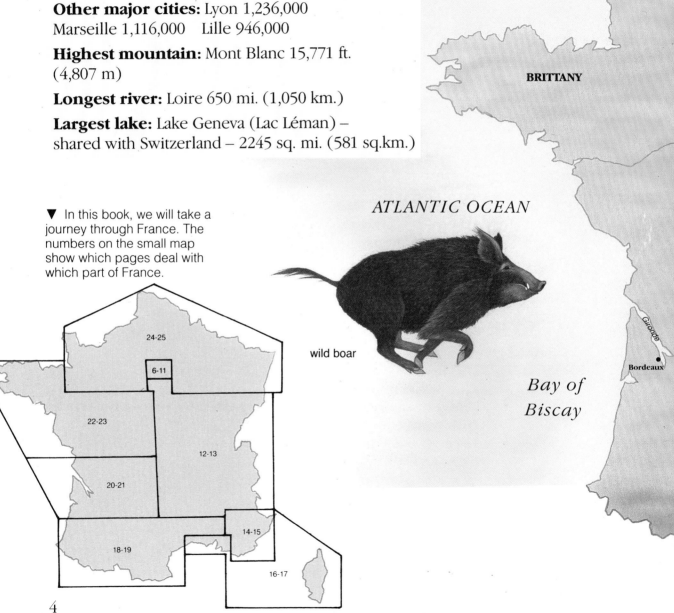

ENGLISH

BRITTANY

ATLANTIC OCEAN

▼ In this book, we will take a
journey through France. The
numbers on the small map
show which pages deal with
which part of France.

24-25

6-11

22-23

12-13

20-21

14-15

18-19

16-17

wild boar

Gironde

Bordeaux

*Bay of
Biscay*

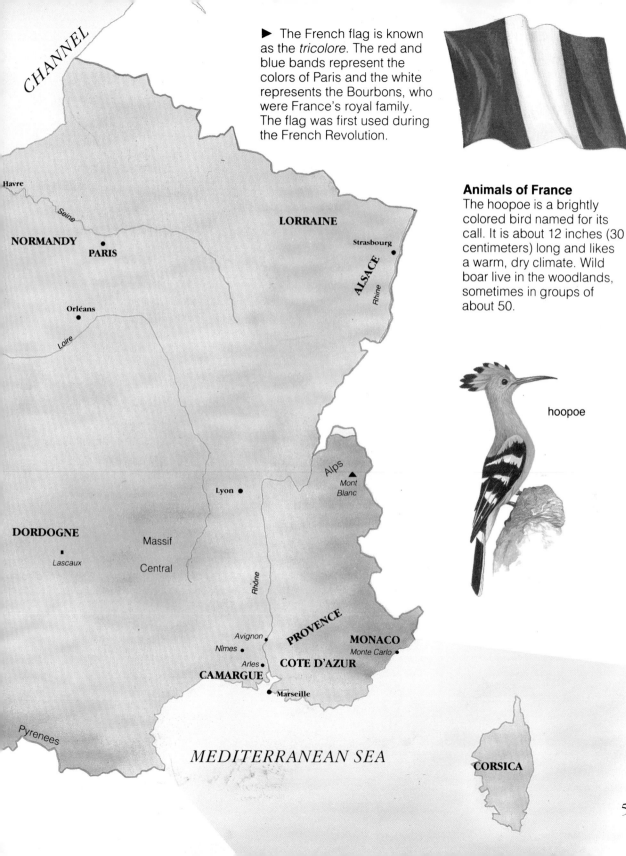

► The French flag is known as the *tricolore*. The red and blue bands represent the colors of Paris and the white represents the Bourbons, who were France's royal family. The flag was first used during the French Revolution.

Animals of France

The hoopoe is a brightly colored bird named for its call. It is about 12 inches (30 centimeters) long and likes a warm, dry climate. Wild boar live in the woodlands, sometimes in groups of about 50.

hoopoe

CHANNEL

Havre

Seine

NORMANDY

PARIS

LORRAINE

Strasbourg

ALSACE

Rhine

Orléans

Loire

Alps

Mont Blanc

Lyon

DORDOGNE

Massif

Central

Lascaux

Rhône

Avignon

Nîmes

Arles

PROVENCE

MONACO

Monte Carlo

COTE D'AZUR

CAMARGUE

Marseille

Pyrenees

MEDITERRANEAN SEA

CORSICA

5

Welcome to France

French people often call their country the hexagon because it has six sides. On five of these sides are seas or mountains. The northern part of the country is often cold and rainy, whereas the south is hot and dry for most of the year, but with violent storms. The east has peaks on which the snow never melts, while the west has many broad, fertile plains. The lifestyles of the people vary from region to region, too.

Almost 2,000 years ago the Romans conquered Gaul, as they called it, and stayed for 500 years. Gaul was then invaded by a Germanic tribe called the Franks, which is how the country got its modern name.

▶ A stall at an outdoor market where you can buy white or purple garlic grown in the Provence region of southern France. A string of garlic lasts a long time!

▼ Rural France — a small village with houses built from local stone standing close together. Villages like this are scattered all over the countryside.

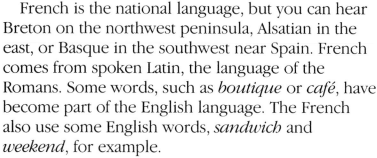

▲ People enjoying the sunshine and conversation over a cup of coffee at an outdoor café in Paris.

French is the national language, but you can hear Breton on the northwest peninsula, Alsatian in the east, or Basque in the southwest near Spain. French comes from spoken Latin, the language of the Romans. Some words, such as *boutique* or *café*, have become part of the English language. The French also use some English words, *sandwich* and *weekend*, for example.

France is one of the leading agricultural nations in Europe, but it has many other successful industries such as aircraft, train, and car manufacturing. It is known throughout the world for its food, art, fashion, and perfume.

It is easy to journey through France by plane, car, train, bicycle, on horseback, or on foot. If you travel on the *autoroutes* (superhighways), you should have money ready for tolls. The *franc* is the unit of French money, divided into 100 *centimes*.

On the banks of the Seine

Paris, the capital of France, is one of the most popular cities in the world. Millions of tourists flock there each year to see its famous sights and enjoy its special atmosphere. Paris got its name from the Celtic tribe, the *Parisii*, who settled there in the 3rd century B.C.

You can take a taxi, a bus, or the subway (*métro*), but the best way to see Paris is on foot. You can wander down broad boulevards, through quiet public gardens, up winding cobbled streets, or along the banks of the Seine River.

▶ Paris is famous for both old and modern buildings. The Grand Arch is a striking example of modern architecture.

▼ A trip along the Seine on a *bâteau mouche* (tourist boat) with Notre Dame in the background. The cathedral of Notre Dame was built on the Ile de la Cité, an island in the Seine.

A boat ride down the Seine will show you many sights. The Louvre is one of the largest and richest museums in the world. It used to be a royal palace, but now it contains many priceless works of art. The most famous is the *Mona Lisa*, painted by the Italian artist, Leonardo da Vinci, at the beginning of the 16th century. The Louvre did not have enough space to exhibit all its possessions, so in the 1980s an underground extension was built where you enter through a glass pyramid in the courtyard.

A little further down the Seine you come to the most famous site of all — the Eiffel Tower. You can take an elevator to the top for a bird's-eye view of Paris.

The Latin Quarter is well worth a visit. It is a lively student area with many cinemas, theaters, and cafés. The Sorbonne, France's oldest university founded in the 12th century, is in this quarter. The students were once taught only in Latin, which is how the area got its name.

▲ The world-famous Eiffel Tower floodlit at night.

A trip into history

A 15-minute train ride from the center of Paris takes you to the town of Versailles. There you can visit a magnificent palace with beautiful gardens. It was here that the kings of France lived.

The longest-serving and most powerful king was Louis XIV, who was only four years old when he came to the throne in 1643. He was known as the Sun King, because he lived a life of great luxury. He tried to control everything in France, and was hated by many people.

Back in Paris, you can go to a play at the *Comédie Française*. This is the magnificent theater that Louis XIV built to honor his favorite playwright, Molière. France is famous for its many great writers. In the 18th century another author, Voltaire, was imprisoned twice in the Bastille for criticizing the government.

► The magnificent palace of Versailles was built by Louis XIV. He was anxious to keep any possible rivals under his eye, so he had to build a palace large enough to house them all. You can visit the palace today, but it is almost empty because everything inside was stolen or destroyed during the French Revolution.

▼ This 19th-century painting shows Napoleon leading his army to another battle where he hoped to increase the size of his empire. The leaders rode horses, but the soldiers had to march many miles.

▲ The Arc de Triomphe is a great memorial. Today it is surrounded by fast-moving cars!

You can take the *métro* from the theater to the Bastille. The prison doesn't exist anymore, but there is a monument to celebrate what is for most French people the greatest event in their history. On July 14, 1789, the poor people stormed the prison and set the prisoners free. They no longer wanted to be ruled by a king. They wanted to choose a ruler who would care more about them. This was the beginning of the French Revolution. Four years later, Louis XVI was taken prisoner and executed. Many of his supporters were also killed.

For a pleasant evening walk in Paris, stroll up the Champs Elysées. This is a long, broad boulevard, one of the grandest in the world. At one end you will see the *Arc de Triomphe*, which looks impressive in the lights. This huge arch was built on the orders of the famous general Napoleon Bonaparte to celebrate his many victorious battles. Napoleon seized power soon after the French Revolution and created an empire, but was finally defeated at the Battle of Waterloo in 1815.

Today France is a republic. The French elect a president who lives in the Elysée Palace in the center of Paris.

On the high-speed train

You can travel from Paris to Lyon on the TGV (*Train à Grande Vitesse*), a high-speed train. It covers the 280-mile (450-kilometer) journey in just two hours. The TGV is the fastest train in the world.

Lyon is a major French city and growing international center. It was founded by the Romans in 43 B.C. and became the capital of Gaul. During the summer you can see a play or concert performed in the Roman amphitheater.

Although there are many modern buildings in Lyon, it has one section with houses that are hundreds of years old. Many of these houses are linked by passages opening into courtyards. You can walk a long way without ever using the streets.

Lyon is in the Rhône Valley between two mountainous regions, the Alps and the Massif Central. If you travel west you are soon on the Massif Central plateau, where you can walk or ride a horse across some of the most uninhabited countryside of France.

▲ In the old part of the town of Le Puy, there is an extraordinary 400 feet (125-meter) high pinnacle — the remains of a former volcano. Right on the top is a cathedral.

▲ The Massif Central stretches for miles. It is a bleak area, covered by snow in winter, but it is somewhere you can travel for a whole day without meeting anyone.

◄ The TGV network is spreading all over France, making rail travel an efficient method of transportation. The trains are comfortable, reliable, and, of course, extremely fast.

An hour-long drive east from Lyon takes you into the Alps. Here you can see Mont Blanc, the highest mountain in Europe at 15,771 feet (4,807 meters). You can take a cablecar to the top and ski down glaciers and through pine trees to the valley below. The mountain is on the border between France and Italy, and beneath it runs a tunnel over seven miles (12 kilometers) long.

The skiing industry has made many of the Alpine towns and villages wealthy, but in recent years there hasn't always been enough snow. At some resorts they spray water into the cold mountain air so that it falls as snow.

The beautiful blue coast

The Alps descend steadily almost to the Mediterranean coast. This is the region of Provence, beautiful hilly countryside with olive groves, vineyards, and picturesque villages. A typical town is Grasse, the center of the French perfume industry. Roses, jasmine, lavender, and bitter orange blossom grow in the fields around the town. The flowers are picked and distilled to make some of the most expensive perfume in the world.

During the summer there are frequent forest fires in Provence. The vegetation is very dry and fires can spread quickly especially if the *mistral* is blowing. The mistral is a wind that blows from the north down the Rhône Valley and can last for several days.

Provence is an excellent region for cycling, as long as you don't mind a few hills! Cycling is very popular in France, especially on weekends in the country. Every year people line the streets to cheer on the cyclists in the *Tour de France*, the most famous bicycle race in the world. Over a hundred of the world's best cyclists spend about three weeks racing 2,500 miles (4,000 kilometers) through the plains, towns, and mountains of France.

The Côte d'Azur, or Azure Coast, named for the clear blue sky, stretches from the Italian border to Marseille. Cycling along the coast, you can admire the beauty of the deep blue sea and the dark red rocks.

14

◄ A clutch of cyclists racing through the countryside of France on one of the stages of the *Tour de France*.

▼ The color of the sky and the sea of the Mediterranean at Nice show why this area is called the Côte d'Azur. The climate is very warm so palm trees and many bright and beautiful plants grow here.

The mountain in the sea

If you take the coast road from the Italian border, you will soon come to the tiny principality of Monaco. It is an independent state, ruled by a prince, but it is protected by France. Here you will find the town of Monte Carlo, famous for its casinos, the annual car rally that ends there, and the Grand Prix motor race held in its streets.

Marseille is the biggest city on the Mediterranean coast. It is France's largest commercial port, and has a large shipbuilding industry. The French national anthem, the "Marseillaise," was first sung in Paris by soldiers from Marseille during the French Revolution.

◄ A fisherman at the Vieux Port, or Old Port, at Marseille lays out the morning's catch for sale. At the front of the table he is selling fish that would make good soup and at the back he has a box of red mullet.

A boat trip of a few hours takes you from Marseille to the island of Corsica, which belongs to France. It is sometimes known as "the mountain in the sea," as it is covered with pine-laden mountains. The land in the valleys is not very fertile, but most of the island's income comes from tourists. Corsicans are very proud of their island.

Further along the coast is the Camargue. This is a beautiful regional park of marshes and shallow lagoons. One of the best ways to see it is on horseback. You will be able to see black bulls and gray horses roaming free, egrets, beavers, water turtles, and pink flamingoes.

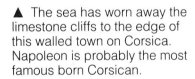

▲ The sea has worn away the limestone cliffs to the edge of this walled town on Corsica. Napoleon is probably the most famous born Corsican.

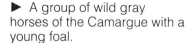

► A group of wild gray horses of the Camargue with a young foal.

Different sides of the hexagon

Near the Camargue are three ancient towns —
Avignon, Nîmes, and Arles. In Avignon you can visit
the magnificent *Palais des Papes*, or Papal Palace,
which is the dramatic setting for plays and concerts
during the summer. From 1309 to 1377 the popes
lived in Avignon, which is why the Palace is so
named. You can also see the famous bridge
mentioned in the song "*Sur le pont d'Avignon*" but
now it only goes halfway across the Rhône River! It
was built in the 12th century, but half of it was swept
away by floods 300 years ago and another bridge was
built.

Both Nîmes and Arles have arenas, built by the
Romans, in which bullfights are sometimes held.
Some of the bulls come from the Camargue.

Summers are very hot in the south of France, so
you may want to sit in the shade of a café terrace and
watch a game of *boules*, which is something like
bowling. Café life is very important in France. It is a
place to play cards or dominoes, to meet friends, or
simply to sit and think.

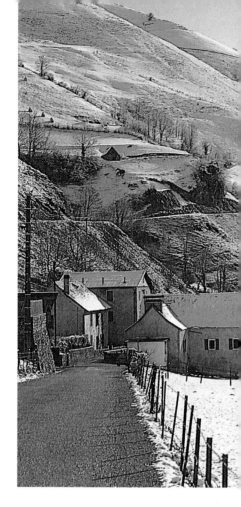

▼ A view of the famous
bridge at Avignon.

◀ A village in the snow-covered mountains of the Pyrenees, in the Basque region of France.

▼ These children are dressed in traditional costume to take part in a folk festival. These festivals are held during the summer to keep music and dance from the region alive.

One side of the hexagon of France is formed by the Pyrenees mountain range, which divides France from Spain. The people in the western part of this area are Basques, and they share a language with their Spanish neighbors on the other side of the mountains. Many tourists visit the Pyrenees year-round for skiing and walking vacations.

Driving up the Atlantic coast, you will see that it is different from the Mediterranean. Here huge waves come crashing down onto the broad, tidal beaches. The coast is quite straight and can be dangerous for swimmers, but it is a good surfing coast. Expert surfers from all over the world gather on this coast for summer competitions.

19

Forests, vineyards, and cave paintings

Southwest of Bordeaux lies the region called the Landes, which has the largest forest in France. You can walk, cycle, or ride through countless miles of pine trees.

To the north and east of Bordeaux the countryside opens out into vineyards. There are grapevines everywhere, in fields and over the hills. They are planted in long, straight lines, stretching as far as the eye can see. If your journey takes you through this area in autumn, it will be the time when the grapes are picked.

▶ A painting of a black cow from the Lascaux caves in the Dordogne region. The paintings are a fascinating record of the animals that lived in the region 15,000 years ago.

▼ Vineyards on the grounds of the Château Monbazillac are growing grapes that will be made into a sweet, white wine.

A little further inland, in the Dordogne region, is the place where over fifty years ago four boys searching for their dog made a magnificent discovery. They found the dog in a large cave, which had several galleries leading from it. On the walls were beautifully colored paintings of real and mythical animals. Archeologists date the paintings at over 15,000 years old, and believe that the cave was used for hunting ceremonies. You cannot visit this cave at Lascaux anymore, but you can see replicas at a nearby cave. There are many other fascinating caves to be visited in this area.

cheese

Famous châteaux

From Bordeaux, you can take the train north to Tours, which lies on France's longest river, the Loire. You can row or canoe down the Loire and see the famous châteaux. These are beautiful country houses built hundreds of years ago for the French nobility. Few of them are furnished, but they are striking from a distance. During the summer months at some of the bigger châteaux you can see *son et lumière* performances, in which the history of the châteaux and their owners is acted out with sound and lighting effects.

▲ The rugged coastline of Brittany near the most westerly part of France. During winter these rocks are often battered by great waves.

◄ The château of Azay-le-Rideau is built on the banks of the Indre, a tributary of the Loire. It was built at the water's edge, and its image is reflected in the water.

► Joan of Arc, dressed to lead the French army to victory against the English during the Hundred Years' War.

A boat trip up the Loire will take you to Orléans. This was where France's greatest national heroine, Joan of Arc, led the army that defeated the English during the Hundred Years' War. The Maid of Orléans, as she is also known, was captured and burned at the stake in 1431. The brave peasant girl was declared a saint almost 500 years later, in 1920.

Traveling westward from Orléans, you come to Brittany. The countryside and coast are rugged, often swept by strong winds and storms from the Atlantic Ocean. In Brittany, there is a strong feeling of independence from the rest of France. There is a Breton language, although today most Bretons speak French, and many of the place names are quite different from those in other parts of the country. There is a national costume that many of the older people wear on special days. Pancakes, with a variety of fillings, called *galettes*, and cider are the local specialties.

Near the town of Carnac in Brittany you can see megaliths, or huge stones. Some are standing, and others lie flat. They were put there by people who lived in the area thousands of years ago.

The industrial north

A trip along the north coast of France brings you to the beaches of Normandy. It was here on June 6, 1944 that British and American forces landed to liberate France from Germany during the Second World War. The Allies were joined by French forces led by General Charles de Gaulle, and eventually the German army was defeated. De Gaulle later became President of France.

Le Havre is the second largest French port. It is very important because it is linked to Paris by the Seine River and has direct access to the Atlantic Ocean.

Further east, the area near the Belgian border was once a booming industrial region, especially for steel, coal, and textiles. In the last 40 years, however, many factories have had to close because the country didn't need what they produced. Many people lost their jobs. Now there is new hope for the north because it's been recently linked to Paris by a high-speed train and will be linked to England by a tunnel beneath the English Channel. These links should create jobs and income in the area.

▲ England and France meet for the first time under the Channel in the newly dug tunnel. Trains will link the two countries under the sea.

◄ A container ship is being loaded at Le Havre. Containers are lifted by crane onto huge ships which then take French goods all over the world.

The north coast was also the scene of fighting between the Western Allies and the Germans during the First World War (1914-1918). You can visit trenches that have been maintained as a monument to those killed in that war.

As you travel toward Strasbourg, through the regions of Lorraine and Alsace, you will notice that many places have German names. These regions belonged to Germany at different times in their history.

Strasbourg is just west of the Rhine River, which forms the border between France and Germany. You will notice the German influence in the buildings and food. In Strasbourg you can visit the European Parliament. France was one of the founding members of the European Economic Community.

▲ Mont St. Michel is one of the most visited sites in France. The rock stands 500 feet (150 meters) above sea level. On the top is an abbey, built in the 11th century, as well as a fortress, a small town, and a monastery. The rock is linked to the mainland by a causeway. At high tide it is surrounded by the sea and at low tide by dangerous sands. It is said that the tide comes in around Mont St. Michel faster than a galloping horse.

France around the world

When you return to Paris, your journey is not over yet. You can fly thousands of miles across the Atlantic Ocean to the Caribbean islands of Martinique and Guadeloupe, or south to Réunion Island in the Indian Ocean. These are just three of the lands that were conquered by France in the past. You can walk through sugar and banana plantations, stroll along beaches lined with coconut palms, or see tropical rain forests.

Other countries once ruled by France are now independent, but in many of them French remains an official language. Algeria, in North Africa, fought an eight-year war with France before gaining its independence in 1962.

Many people from these ex-colonies have settled in France to find a better life. Others are political refugees, seeking safety from injustice in their own countries. You will see people from many different countries in France.

On your journey you have seen that France has a varied climate, landscape, and population. It is a country that you can visit again and again and still discover something new. *Au revoir!*

▶ These French children are enjoying a day out. In a group like this there are probably many children whose families came from the other countries which have strong links with France.

▼ Martinique depends on tourism. Most of its inhabitants are very poor — in stark contrast to the tourists.

▶ Sugar cane is one of the main crops in Martinique and Guadeloupe.

Fact file

Education

French children start elementary school when they are six, but many of them go to preschool from the age of two. They stay at elementary school for five years until they are eleven. The day in most French elementary schools lasts from nine in the morning to four in the afternoon, apart from Wednesday, which is a half-day. Some schools close all day on Wednesday but open on Saturday morning. Eleven-year-olds move to secondary school. Many children leave school when they are 16, but some choose to stay on until 18 or 19 to attempt a series of exams called the *baccalauréat*. If you pass these exams you can go to one of the 70 universities in France. French children have a long day at school with a lot of homework, and short vacations at Christmas and Easter, but they have a long vacation of over two months in the summer.

Industry

France's main industries are the production of cars, textiles, electronic goods, and chemicals. Its aeronautical industry is expanding rapidly. France's energy used to come from the coal mined in the northeast and gas from the foothills of the Pyrenees, but it is now relying more and more on nuclear power.

Agriculture

France is self-sufficient. This means that it can produce enough food to feed its population without having to buy from other countries if necessary. There are few other countries in Europe that could do this. The main crops are wheat and corn, vegetables such as potatoes, and fruit such as grapes, apples, peaches, and apricots. In coastal areas fishing is an important industry, and in the mountains there is a great deal of forestry.

Language

French developed from the Latin spoken in Gaul in Roman times. French is spoken in Belgium, Luxembourg, and parts of Switzerland, as well as in France and its colonies and former colonies. Try using some French words.

Bonjour	Hello
Merci	Thank you
S'il vous plaît	Please
Ça va?	How are you?
Très bien, merci	Very well, thank you

► A nuclear power station at Chinon. Nuclear power supplies more than half the energy needs of France. France is a world leader in the development of nuclear power and technology.

▼ The flamingoes of the Camargue live further north than any other flamingoes. They eat shrimp and nest on the islands around the water. Their nests look like mud pies! When they are in flight they make a tremendous amount of noise which, combined with their color, makes a stunning sight.

Literature

France is famous for its literature and French people are proud of their writers. Montaigne wrote learned essays and Rabelais wrote exciting stories in the 16th century. The 17th century is famous for the playwrights Corneille, Molière, and Racine and the 18th century for the philosophers Voltaire, Rousseau, and Diderot. Balzac, Flaubert, and Zola were novelists and Baudelaire and Rimbaud famous poets of the 19th century. The best known writers of this century are Jean-Paul Sartre and Albert Camus.

Food

French people enjoy cooking and eating. Sunday lunch is an important part of family life when several generations may come together to enjoy a good meal. During the week, however, people eat simpler meals. They tend to have a small breakfast of coffee and bread or *croissants*. Many have a large lunch, but for most the main meal of the day is in the evening. This usually includes meat and vegetables, followed by a green salad, cheese, and finally fruit or a sweet dessert. A vital part of each meal is the long loaves of bread you see people carrying home all over France.

▼ Parts of this magnificent castle at Fougères in Brittany date from the 12th century. The massive walls and thirteen towers have seen many battles and seiges since then.

▼ The European Parliament building at Strasbourg. Elected representatives from the countries of the European Economic Community meet here to debate and decide policy for the Community.

Boules

Boules is one of the national games of France. During the summer in every town and village in France you will see people of all ages gathering to play boules. The game varies slightly from region to region, but the object is to throw or roll a heavy aluminum ball, or *boule*, as close as possible to a small wooden ball called a *cochonnet*. Each player has three balls and there are usually two players on a team. The players get a point for each *boule* nearer the *cochonnet* than their opponents', and the first team with thirteen points wins.

B.C.	Time chart
c500	Celts arrive in Gaul.
58	Caesar becomes governor of Gaul.
53-50	Gauls revolt against Romans; their leader, Vercinétorix, surrenders to Caesar.
43	Lugdunum (Lyon) becomes the Roman capital of Gaul.
A.D.	
486	Invasion of Gaul by the Franks, who conquer the whole of Gaul.
800	Charlemagne, king of the Franks, defeats many tribes and rules Holy Roman Empire.
1066	William, Duke of Normandy, conquers England.
1095	First Crusade to the east.
1163	Building begins on Notre Dame cathedral in Paris.
1257	Founding of the Sorbonne as a theological college.
1337-1453	Hundred Years' War with England.
1348	Black Death reaches France.
1429	Joan of Arc liberates Orléans.
1562-1598	Civil wars between Roman Catholics and Huguenots (Protestants).
1598	Edict of Nantes — Protestants are now free to practice their religion.
1643-1715	Reign of Louis XIV.
1648-1653	Revolts against the monarchy.
1667-1714	Wars against Holland, Spain, and Austria.
1789-1799	French Revolution, beginning with the storming of the Bastille (1789).
1793	King Louis XVI beheaded.
1799	Napoleon Bonaparte takes power.
1804-1815	Napoleon is emperor of France.
1804	The Napoleonic Code, a new system of laws, is instituted.
1815	Napoleon defeated at Waterloo; France becomes a monarchy again.
1848	Revolt against the monarchy; Louis-Napoleon (nephew of Napoleon) becomes president.
1852-1870	Louis-Napoleon is emperor.
1870-1871	France is defeated in war with Prussia.
1871	The Paris Commune — a revolutionary government opposed to the peace treaty, rebels; the revolt is crushed by troops.
1885	Louis Pasteur discovers the technique of vaccination.
1889	Eiffel Tower is built for Paris Exposition.
1898	Marie and Pierre Curie discover radioactive radium.
1900	Opening of the Paris *métro*.
1909	Louis Blériot makes the first flight across English Channel.
1914-1918	First World War.
1924	Summer Olympic Games held in Paris. First Winter Olympics held in Chamonix.
1939-1945	Second World War.
1954-1962	The Algerian War; the colony wins independence from France.
1957	Foundation of the European Economic Community.
1968	Revolt against the government, first by students and then by workers; general strike.
1969	President de Gaulle resigns.
1979	First French space flight.
1981	François Mitterrand becomes President.

Index